In an Invisible Glass Case
Which Is Also a Frame

More Praise for Julia Guez

"With great precision, Julia Guez arranges the things of the world into richly imagined tableaux. Guez also beautifully arranges thinking and feeling. Her poems are uncannily tethered to interconnectedness and thresholds. This is a remarkable, keen debut."
—Eduardo C. Corral

"*In an Invisible Glass Case Which Is Also a Frame* is a debut collection that marvels at the full and often unbelievable spectrum of life. In these poems the body becomes a strange chameleon; parenthood an opening to unspeakable joy and terror; and the self a spinning top of equal parts awareness and wildness. Guez moves deftly from the domestic to the political, from the literary to the mundane: any line in this collection is sure to contain a diversity of reference and register that continually surprises and rewards the reader. Marked by intelligence, humor, and empathy, this daring collection is nothing short of an exclamation of living."
—Amy Meng

In an Invisible Glass Case Which Is Also a Frame

Julia Guez

Four Way Books
Tribeca

Library of Congress Cataloging-in-Publication Data
Names: Guez, Julia, author.
Title: In an invisible glass case which is also a frame / Julia Guez.
Description: New York, NY : Four Way Books, [2019]
Identifiers: LCCN 2019004730 | ISBN 9781945588372 (pbk. : alk. paper)
Classification: LCC PS3607.U4716 A6 2019 | DDC 811/.6--dc23
LC record available at https://lccn.loc.gov/2019004730

This book is manufactured in the United States of America and printed on acid-free paper.

Four Way Books is a not-for-profit literary press. We are grateful for the assistance
we receive from individual donors, public arts agencies, and private foundations.

This publication is made possible with public funds from the
National Endowment for the Arts

and from the New York State Council on the Arts, a state agency,

and from the Jerome Foundation.

We are a proud member of the Community of Literary Magazines and Presses.

For
Jean Elizabeth Riopelle Guez
Charles Guez
&
Elizabeth Burchfield Ballard

Contents

One

Two

Three

Look—in this one glass case, a breathless history
Of the unthinkable, each artifact
                    In the shape of a night-finding bluff or
A species that had never been named

—Lucie Brock-Broido

One

Still Life with Vicodin

Maybe there is no magic, no Technicolor,
but inside the seed, there is a kingdom.

Ask me anything, I will tell you the truth.
It is a fatal wound for every wolf and thimble.

Even the night watchman is not immune.
We may as well sing, George.

Inside the throat,
a carriage, a pony, a parachute.

The New Cartography

This is about borage and compline, anything to still the mind.

This is about money, the lack and the brine. It will be epic

To forth a family (hence the boat full of postage, rum, citrus and

Eiderdown for an eventual pillow). Never mind the reed and sedge,

I have a compass and corkscrew, two blankets to keep us warm.

This is not entirely nautical. A lot depends on wind and water, though.

This is also about blood-work, the pageantry of robe and coin,

How we faculty the ocean, re-reading the *Odyssey* alongside *What*

To Expect When You're Expecting, but we're not expecting.

This is about travel then. This is about translation.

On the Airstrip at Tambor, en Route to Monteverde

But I can be unhappy *anywhere*, George.

Nocturne

All but braying, a sadness that animal.

And the walk is a rite wherein
the sadness may, if only

for a moment, forget its many reasons to be
(hence the attention again

to other fields,
where leaves burn by the fence-

posts and the fields further out,
forgetting the leaves altogether and the smell of them).

The walk is a ritual wherein
the scenery exists mostly outside the self.

There is a ridge then below us only ocean,
a kind of shorthand for stillness

born on the back of something else.

Evensong

I

Benumbing but not exactly
Ativan
        (Greek for to quiet

the noisome drone
here and there of the qualms,

my very own
empire of regret
        not wanting to amass

more of itself
and at that, failing).

II

The Atlantic vain with stars and what of its song?

The so on and so forth of a new
        etcetera, flux of sea-

faring elements – how they loll,

7

      the vespered sails

at nighttime, a model.

III

The moon too, and its effects.

Lights across the gulf, a slow color.

The evening palms' view on to the river

dwindling downhill out of habit

more than anything else.

What it has done to bridges before

not what it is doing now.

IV

Ora et labora they say and I am listening still.

What, in the end, the slenderest hands will carry

hours soon reveal. Among other things, a vast

array of antidotes, no two the same:
camphor, mostly, quietude,

or to begin again, the nightly weightlessness.

V

The ocean indifferent to all of this willing onward –

one concavity after another, endlessly inflecting
a small part of sadly

patterns aren't predictive or enduring and they certainly aren't

magical much as the human eye may wish
to believe in some kind of continuing.

Have We Made It Across the Vast Plain of Night?

No.

What It Might've Been Like to Come of Age in the South

The truth, I want to say, is as follows.
But I can't.

The agon often as not
finding

       enough

gentleness and/or humor
to go on

eluding all but the nimblest
interpreter

       whose head now

hangs to one side
on trains

like a stem-cut
flower

       longing for the earth again.

Still Life with *Particularly Distressing Circumstances*

All that work and for what. *His body began to feel*

as if it were entirely liquid. His limbs felt soft and porous.
All he wanted to do was close his eyes.

One convalescence after another, a kind of *willed dying.*

He had felt as if he were in a glass box with fragile walls,
deep in the ocean. If he spoke or moved, he thought,

it would create a vibration, which would cause

the glass to shatter. Then, of course,
the *water would pour in.*

Half-way around the world,

soup, saltines, a back and forth of voices
whose unison might be deafening, if

what has been called a movement consisted of more than this
chorus of deer-like faces

altogether too innocent to know the difference between talk and song is

slight almost imperceptible.
After words have failed "This is a way of saying, 'This is unspeakable,'" but

he had just begun to whisper:

"It will go well for me." "I do not feel alone." "I am not the worst."
Soon, perhaps, he will hum again.

Still Life with Extreme Weather

To the sensate lawns at the perimeter of a lot beyond the boatyard,

the bending in blue dresses to touch something

there and gone, the sod,

wild chicory and golden rod withstanding
most of what is said to follow

the last gingham on the line and everything after that

which New England knows well how to cast

in other colors, as if the fear she will never come back is unfounded.

Epilogue

A cistern full of asters,

notes from the split-risk ward

above the lindens tops of poplars wave

in the long light, an agitation of birds.

What they fever after, I have fevered after—

in tight swaths—circling the only one who makes

all the seasons more beautiful than they really are.

Coming now to the place where no word is

apt, parting.

Still Life with an Opioid Epidemic

This will be one
weaning after another

and so I say
beware the hairpin

made to mean
more once she leaves

the hairpin behind,
orphaning several of them

on the bedside
now and after, all

weep over the smallest things:
the lank of them

lying in rooms
whose walls cough

across the hall
from Mother who

pretends the curtains aren't
crawling. The paint peeling

yawns through the longest
withdrawal, a larghetto:

Infinitesimal feet, the dying
cord, a foreskin,

the sound of that
fist beating against

the bassinette by the fern
and the fern's condolences.

Myth, Then

A willing Anchises I don't know (and by that, I mean a guide or guides).
One underworld for each of us—perhaps the task is to figure it out on our own,

not stop to ask whose shoulders to square the hips on or how
to fit one foot then the next into the palm of a hand belonging to the demi-god

who, shortcomings and all, presumably passed this way before.
No antidote to overthinking—not here, at least: the magpie on the branch above us

colludes with the plenteous palm until we're both conscious of wanting to enjoy this
more than we do, or to enjoy it less abstractly. But the torque of the mind at work,

the din of it trying to order all of this in language—the river we swing alongside,
the hammock and the shade, the humming all of these

18

(as if nothing exists outside of what we name, or exists in a form we fail
to understand without another medium to interpose). Say what hurts then, say

where. Say we only sit and look at the ocean for so long and say why.
The forecast is vast and musical, say. The inverse is also true

especially in situations like this one.
The impulse to catalogue everything finally spent, I know you feel foreign to yourself,

you feel foreign to me as well.
Home is a question of this and that frequency then

something akin to silence—a word for which my lexicon can't supply a cognate,
only gestures, mostly, tokens, a being here together on the same side of this ocean,

the sound canceling itself out across so many distances until
there is nothing other than this

to say, a small aperture opening between the phrases.

Two

Epithalamium

Leave the lily alone and gild the finger.
    Platinum is dactylic, after all.

Moon over Massachusetts, you are so civil.
    You exceed expectation.

We can do without a week in Martinique,
    Glenlivet and cunnilingus:

this is not a film. Besides
    no water need redden into wine.

Still Life with Worsening Income Inequality

A cadence unto something almost metrical interspersed with the sound of several
rivers and at least one bridge—matchstick pylons, multi-colored flags.

A gathering music in those tea-light windows, so many mouths, the prim-
rose platform edge. And collars upturning outside, as if history isn't

a record over and over the same and also a prophecy like any other, foretelling
the obvious danger—these shoulders, the sweep of them,

tightening against the cold before the other night begins.

The World, According to Whitehead

At either end of the continuum
and here too,

keening is easy.

The world, according
to Whitehead, is still

more than amenable

to manifold interpretations—
my own no less valid

because it's fanciful,

although I've considered the facts.

This, Winter

Busy the hands with backgammon,
tell me about the year.

The wifely chamomile and Klonopin
no help, have a saltine.

This is to say, I understand.
Once submersible, I am now a buoy.

Fatigue is the new normal.

For the Mind in the Act of Entertaining Itself,

This is not a gurney.

      We may as well be in a museum. After the intravenous,
confetti and Clindamycin. Sleep then keep sleeping through

the details, all the way through to the part with croquet and cucumber
      on the lawn, all the trappings of Empire,
but none of the pornography.

Katabasis

I

Paperwhites. Here, of all places.

Unlike the others, they will portend

more. Inside of sixty seconds,

a quorum in plain clothes.

Falling to the floor giving way to another floor,

another false canopy.

II

Oysters
in the soil
where a maggot might've been
boring into mealy harpsichords.

III

Frail rights to bend the centrifugal back.

IV

And the weathervanes.
And the water in the bilge of a boat—

Lethe, such a wide river—
the-main-and-mast where exactly, and the thousand oars, the thousand
hands?

V

Down the stairs to the quay, the same washerwoman as before
when what sky there was was not enough.

It's difficult to describe a forest.

And the blind eye blinking at nothing.
And the owls not what they seem.

And the vats of vellum

sacks they fill with candles at the very end.

The dust of them on the lake in the shape of a crater.

And the milky outline of a Virgin back-lit

by a host of gold and green coronas in transit to where

not all the promises would be kept.
And the ledger. A bowl of cigarettes,

wet once and gray all over.

And the tumbrels on another errand—feathers on the starving horses'
red and blue bridles

flouncing.

VI

And the trees which must bleed to speak,

their release from pain only further pain.

And the ferryman, mouth

widening around another egg.

And the nightingale

telling some of what it is to be female:

through and *through*

on a tongue

thickening with red and white twine

asterisks.

Sour wine to sew

the feathers on.

Wretched body, unable to walk or crawl.

The new one set to fly.

VII

And the skylessness unto

a room almost all metal.

And the masquerade.

Mess on the floor

as in Gualeyguachú after a carnival

entire constellations reconfigure themselves

above, as if to mean more.

VIII

And the Klieg lights, a bandoneon, the terrible swing of a censer.

IX

Women I know nothing of

tending to what of me is here after

the sudden *anodos*—

breathing and whatnot while

the selfsame is still

in the Nethermost bemoaning

the wherewithal those days you feel

perfectly inseparable from your own hands.

Lost the dominion of a mind softly

searching for its delinquent palaces.

X

A shade like all the other shades.
        Susceptible to rust and moths.
Maybe taken in the night by thieves.

XI

The fear of these things.
And the solstices.

Advent always ending with the letter, O.

XII

And the mayfly—mouthparts,
a foreleg ahead of the wingéd
emblem threading itself through a narrow
opening in the celluloid.

XIII

And the self—gondolierless yet leavening on a set of invisible strings.

XIV

And the frangipani, but faintly.

XV

And the hand over hand

to bring the self above the body

strewn among Plasticine

reeds and rushes in this

diorama of a bed.

And the foam-core

leopards, two by two.

XVI

Not unlike waking any other day—

the whiteness of those arms

there to receive me, bleeding and but home.

The Quarry Implied by the Monument

In this weather: all
the leafless ampersands
line the boardwalk

beneath a pewter sky.

Boughs of blackbirds keen
uselessly.
The monumentality of this

sadness whose hold once

lessened unto almost nothing
during the day. Believing it
real then only at night—

the force of that

half-light through the curtains.
And the wind,
the sound of it, stirring—

I

A state one may in real desperation induce by subjecting the body to distress
up to and including sleeplessness and/or forbearance from routines in place,
it is clear, for a reason. Also,

II

illusion (one may or may not recognize as such until more and more thorough
attempts to reconcile versions of the same story show themselves to be
irreconcilable at long last, calling the whole process into question). Also,

III

travel. As in, relocation outside the city outside time and time's narrow definitions.
Also, by other means.
Not at all content with increments of more than a few days between

the only ease to offset the rigor of this worrying, a carnal one

the late parade may not fully understand

beginning, as it does, with the red first then yellow hibiscus on the pillow wilting.

IV

The new liturgy, of course, a Northern one.

V

But even here, rings around the bourbon on the bedside pattern themselves like so:

(((*)))   (((*)))

and the effect thereof is reassuring.

VI

Few precedents for what follows the weight of world without end arcs to this untold

VII

tenderness the telling of which is at least one suicide away from the sun-lit

side of the garden where *untold* means not *in the dark*, but *numberless*,

numberless not *without number*, but *many*, the impulse to be not halved

somehow intact after Pentonville after Sachsenhausen,

rain falling through the leaves until the whitest flowers

loosen all at once, that lymph and startle

almost too much for any mathematics to model the groundswell of feeling after.

Paraphrase

From the moon whose many deaths meant only to console us

a faint promise whose absence is no fault of the weather. Outside of this
window a new psalm and therefore a tanager

     which does not belong here

and has, after all the archetypal traumas and then some,

thought of settling in whereabouts vague
and untranslatable, yet never settled

     hardly ever resting, on this branch

beginning to build itself a home out of what we know

to call kindling, in the cicatrix of a crepe myrtle which
from time to time will flourish

     so completely, the fact of its own

withering is lost among the boughs' pomp and color.

The Dark Showed Me a Face

Where the moons are fuller, the pull of them felt different before.
When what tides there were affected us alone.

A wood—more like a stand of tree-like colorations—the light entirely other than:

West again to the river, a wall there following the river as if according to plan.
Each new coordinate east of the one they say is gentlest.

Apt even for offspring.

Nearness be that mark where every bell but one may be broken for awhile.
I swear I can see the square from here—

the pigeons and the wish-filled fountains.

Self-Portrait as a New Moon

Rag in the mouth of the monk-like
telephone, loupe
to see the tail-feather of a swan

blackening the calfskin,
I work alone in the lampless
scriptorium.

Still anonymous
yet to bulge at the plait,
unmistakable.

I'm still demurring. But
soon you'll know my signature
among people, or on the skin.

Still Life in Another Neighborhood We Can't Afford

Pearl-lined with a lace stratagem
the day's asleep in drag on the sofa.
Come upon sheets in the courtyard.
Blue first then yellow irises out front.
A park whose piers secret away a song
only fish and the drowned know to sing:
luchando, luchando, luchando.
They say no wharfage here and mean it.
Grass painted green. Living rooms full
of Lucian Freud. No sequins in the window
on the corner, only a few flags—none of them
mauve with sea-foam rings. All
the Dominicans are leaving. I repeat,
all the Dominicans are leaving.

Three

Ambiguous Gifts, as What Gods Give Must Be

And the reason for this, the reasons

to feel more of it than we think

owe much, in our case,
to Kalder and Brahms,

Kistler's   Cuvée

Elizabeth and sex with the same person

over a period of many years—
owing also to sores,

odors, nausea, aging,   gravity,

every last schism between

our physical wills and our actual
capacities:

the fact or facts of having   a body

defining itself more broadly

as the province of another body
hence the colics and the fluxes

and the fevers,   then awe soon

to break us open wide

to the body's other ranges—

Idyll

In the corner of my unquiet, there's a loom.
Behind the loom, undoing.

Let us focus then on the loom.

The tapestry is a kind of omen.
Materials are obviously important.

In the absence of a proper skein, I'm

also a fan of vinyl and feather
intertwined to form a door

opening onto a field

where the saffron is symbolic.
The field is probably a plain.

Nein, a meadow.

See, for example, the lark and the lily.
Watch the hands at work on the herringbone.

They seem to know exactly what to do, weaving

filament and wisteria into a scene—
all very pastoral, unlikely.

There's not one poplar in sight.

There's no dread.
In the corner of the loom, I can see the future,

a face almost

fully-formed. There,
beneath the pear tree in the arbor,

you've never seen anything so beautiful.

Unable to Find What I Was Formerly Sure Was There

This is my body.

Greenery where before there was amnion,
pearl, pollen and salt.

Not that there hasn't also been wonder.
And the effect of many suns setting at once.
A pall we begin by

pretending not to notice.

The first of many deaths,
a martyring:

Anything to bring cantering
back from what river
crossing cold, first

a mare-like plodding sound,

then something more hopeful.
The terrain we travel

lanternlessly and, yes, afraid

won't cohere much longer.
Beyond any semblance of a tree-line

beleaguered by the same thought,

the swale and copse have begun
to bend

birdlessly
abandoning the fallows'
odd interval until pine and juniper disappear

completely.

And sheer, the land mostly tectonic now
has risen to the level of my hands

forcing a final genuflection of sorts.
Ambivalences (and there were some
whose only safe passage had to have been

a violent one),

unmoored
like so many forgotten trades

littering the inlet with hulls.
The saddest wicker paint peeling
nets and phlegm

sound of that last anchor

borne aloft hand over hand, dangling,
the ferryman aware of what this might mean.

Practice telling the story as if
this part's already happened—
the quickening through tissue and bone,

bloodied,

lowering into the bulge of that last
hold. Like a chute—some say,

a tunnel or a toboggan.
The doctor's gown even greener than before
they swarm the buxom Equatorial one—

head bent, body curled—

a creaturely sound
from the vast, void-like and watery

opening out, the throat
a conduit for this
otherworldly force like a glacier

calving

inside the more
obsolete sound of a trireme

that'll always be
circumnavigating
that glacier, gloved

hands holding my own

heels high for the pelvissing
plosive

head, shoulders, hip, knees
feet and cord
that voice never not

in my ear and soon another,

voices
so large in their beautiful Latin,

how could they accept
being refracted so small
in another grammar?

The science of a single pin

piercing
languagelessly through the newest

triad—
a foaling not unlike any other—
diaphanous, indestructible

tether

composed like them of eros,
dust, algebra and fire.

One of Several Plots Against Our Lamblike Son or Daughter

Born wearing only an amulet,
a talisman they take by force,

foreshadowing.

Even here, hands empty
and odd how sickly

without

being specific you long
for a makeshift return to wombwater.

Instead

they give you a glarebox—
the opposite of Mother, if there is one.

They take your wings.
Then they take your shield.

Claim,

Both are vestigial anyway. Claim,

Both belong to the shears.

This is all

part of a dream, of course,
recurring and also a parable.

We will be asked to pretend many things.

To Wear When No One Is Looking,

the seamstress here (a hologram soon obsolete as the last) fashions
me a balsa wood bodice and wings, silk and bullion. We dress these

wounds in iodine and organza, walk again through the same doors
not the same at all when seen from this vantage.

Concerning This New Fear Something Else Will Befall You—
Which, Of Course, It Will—And What Then

Acknowledgments

Many thanks to the following magazines where some of this work has previously appeared (sometimes in slightly different form): *Anamesa; Apogee; Argos Books Calendar (2018); Boston Review; Death Hums; DIAGRAM; Foundry Journal; Hyperallergic; Lambda Literary; No, Dear; Phantom Limb; Springhouse; The Literary Review; Vinyl; Washington Square,* and *92Y's Words We Live In.*

Many thanks to the following writers, editors and artists for necessary insight and encouragement along the way: Emily Brandt, Jennifer Cayer, Alex Cuff, Iris Cushing, Elizabeth Clark Wessel, Joey DeJesus, Jay Deshpande, Thomas Dooley, Joshua Daniel Edwin, Nalini Edwin, Natalie Eilbert, Miranda Field, Jameson Fitzpatrick, Kelly Forsythe, Alina Gregorian, Eamon Grennan, Edith Grossman, Beth Harrison, Gary Hawkins, Richard Howard, Dennis Huston, Cora Jacobs, John James, Brandon Kreitler, Heather Lang, Jessica Laser, Kat Laskowski, Paul Legault, Katie Longofano, Peter Longofano, Ricardo Maldonado, Olivia Luisa Mardwig, Ander Monson, Craig Morgan Teicher, Jerome Murphy, Elizabeth Onusko, Michael Parrish, Allyson Paty, Emma Ramey, Sam Ross, Brian Russell, Eleanor Sarasohn, Jimin Seo, Soren Stockman, Katherine Sullivan, Kate Thorpe, Elizabeth Tubergen, Phillip Williams, Wendy Xu, Samantha Zighelboim and Rachel Zucker.

For what frames this collection, for the epigraph, for the collage and for the gift of working together, my thanks again and again to Lucie Brock-Broido and Mark Strand. For the photography, my thanks to Wesley Mann. For perspective on what this work means to be at its very best, many thanks to Kaveh Akbar, Eduardo C. Corral, Timothy Donnelly, Amy Meng and Camille Rankine. And for the art and animation, my thanks to Bianca Stone.

Many thanks to everyone at Four Way Books: Mari Coates, Clarissa Long, Ryan Murphy and Martha Rhodes.

Thanks to my colleagues at Teach For America New York: Priscilla Forsyth, Myra Gupta, Raiza Lisboa, Aarti Marajh, Reuben Ogbonna, Fanny Spencer and Yeimmy Torrez.

Many thanks to my teachers and to my students.

Thanks, finally, to my family here and abroad: my mother and father, my brothers, my aunts, uncles and cousins, my niece and my nephew; thanks to my mother-in-law, my father-in-law, my brother-in-law and my sister-in-law; and thanks, most of all, to my wife and sons.

Notes

Have We Made It Across the Vast Plain of Night?

[aequus] a smooth or level surface, expanse, surface; a level stretch of
ground, plain; *inmensumne noctis aequor confecimus*? have we made it across
the vast plain of night? the surface of the sea especially as considered as calm
and flat, a part of the sea, a sea; *per aperta volans aequora* soaring over the
open sea; the waters of a river, lake, sea; *tibi rident aequora ponti* the waters
of the sea laugh up at you.

Anne Carson, *NOX*

What It Might've Been Like To Come of Age in the South

The truth, I would like to say here, is as follows. But I can't.

Renata Adler, *Speedboat*

Still Life with *Particularly Distressing Circumstances*

Italics in the poem idicate direct quotations from Rachel Aviv's reporting for
"The Trauma of Facing Deportation," *The New Yorker,* April, 3, 2017.

Still Life with Extreme Weather

No soldiers in the scenery,
No thoughts of people now dead,
As they were fifty years ago,
Young and living in a live air,
Young and walking in the sunshine,

Bending in blue dresses to touch something,
Today the mind is not part of the weather.

Wallace Stevens, "A Clear Day and No Memories," *The Palm at the End of the Mind*

Epilogue

Above the lindens tops of poplars waved
in an old French story, according to Henry
who shook himself & shaved,
rid of that dream. Rid slowly of all his dreams
he faced the wicked ordinary day
in a tumult of seems.

John Berryman, "178", *Dream Songs*

Epithalamium II

My only mistake was that I confined myself so exclusively to the trees of what seemed to me the sun-lit side of the garden, and shunned the other side for its shadow and its gloom. Failure, disgrace, poverty, sorrow, despair, suffering, tears even, the broken words that come from lips in pain, remorse that makes one walk on thorns, conscience that condemns, self-abasement that punishes, the misery that puts ashes on its head, the anguish that chooses sack-cloth for its raiment and into its own drink puts gall:--all these were things of which I was afraid. And as I had determined to know nothing of them, I was forced to taste each of them in turn, to feed on them, to have for a season, indeed, no other food at all.

Oscar Wilde, *De Profundis*

They are untold: the advantages of entangling
oneself completely in a place like this, up and beyond
all chance of discovery, here where *untold* means
not *in the dark*, but *numberless, numberless* not
without number, but *many*—and if I sit in the dark
now and wait without number, the difference is

I do it voluntarily…

Timothy Donnelly, "In His Tree," *The Cloud Corporation*

Katabasis

The day
en route to darkness. The guillotine
on the way to the neck. The train
to nudity. The bus
to being alone. The main-and-mast,
and the thousand oars, the
thousand hands.

Laura Kasischke, "Space, between humans & gods," *Space, in Chains*

What wind there was
What sky there was was not
enough, I could not
hear beyond a cry a signal

Joanna Klink, "River in Dusk," *Circadian*

Stopped mid-motion in the middle
Of what we call a life, I looked up and saw no sky—
Only a dense cage of leaf, tree and twig. I was lost.

It's difficult to describe a forest:
Savage, arduous, extreme in its extremity. I think
And the facts come back, then the fear comes back.

Death, I think, can only be slightly more bitter.

Dante, "Canto I," *Inferno* (Translated by Mary Jo Bang)

My situation appears to me as follows: I speak in a curious, detached manner, and don't necessarily hear myself. I'm grateful for small mercies. Whether anyone follows me I can't tell.

Are you there? If so I'm blind and deaf to you, or you are me, or both're both. One may be imaginary; I've had stranger ideas. I hope I'm a fiction without real hope. Where there's a voice there's a speaker.

I see I see myself as a halt-stop narrative: first person, tiresome. Pronoun sans ante or precedent, warrant or respite. Surrogate for the substantive; contentless form, interestless principle; blind eye blinking at nothing. Who am I. A little *crise d'identite* for you.

I must compose myself.

John Barth, *Autobiography: A Self-Recorded Fiction*

That was the year…when I was discovering that not all of the promises would be kept, that some things are in fact irrevocable and that it had counted after all, every evasion and every procrastination, every mistake, every word, all of it.

Joan Didion, "Goodbye To All That," *Slouching Towards Bethlehem*

The cry of faithlessness is the cry of the damned like Dante's souls locked in trees that must bleed to speak, their release from pain only further pain.

Christian Wiman, "God's Truth Is Life," *My Bright Abyss: Meditation of a Modern Believer*

A loss of something ever felt I —
The first that I could recollect
Bereft I was — of what I knew not
Too young that any should suspect

A Mourner walked among the children
I notwithstanding went about
As one bemoaning a Dominion
Itself the only Prince cast out —

Elder, Today, a session wiser
And fainter, too, as Wiseness is —
I find myself still softly searching
For my Delinquent Palaces —

And a Suspicion, like a Finger
Touches my Forehead now and then

That I am looking oppositely
For the site of the Kingdom of Heaven —

Emily Dickinson, "A loss of something ever felt I—," *The Poems of Emily Dickinson*

The Quarry Implied by the Monument

Dusk returns all in silhouette, a lessening
uncounted though it collects like grain in a silo
or the quarry implied by the monument.
What is returned is the loss. Here—I offer it to you.

Brandon Kreitler, "IX," *Dusking*

The Dark Showed Me a Face

In the sparrow, happy on gravel;
In the winter-wasp, pulsing its wings in the sunlight;
I have been somewhere else; I remember the sea-faced uncles.
I hear, clearly, the heart of another singing,
Lighter than bells,
Softer than water.

Wherefore, O birds and small fish, surround me.
Lave me, ultimate waters.
The dark showed me a face.
My ghosts are all gay.
The light becomes me.

Theodore Roethke, "Praise to the End!", *Praise to the End!*

Self-Portrait as a New Moon

to understand *epidemic,*
epidermis begin *among, on,*

near to, or *in addition,* as in
among people, or *on the skin.*

Brian Teare, "Of Paradise and the Structure of Gardens," *Pleasure*

Ambiguous Gifts, as What Gods Give Must Be

Imagine, then, by miracle with me,
(Ambiguous gifts, as what gods give must be)
What could not possibly be there,
And learn a style from a despair.

William Empson, "The Last Pain," *The Complete Poems*

World is crazier and more of it than we think,
Incorrigibly plural. I peel and portion
A tangerine and spit the pips and feel
The drunkenness of things being various.

Louis MacNeice, "Snow," *Collected Poems*

There's a great deal that's bad about having a body. If this is not so obviously true that no one needs examples, we can just quickly mention pain, sores, odors, nausea, aging, gravity, sepsis, clumsiness, illness, limits — every last schism between our physical wills and our actual capacities.

Can anyone doubt we need help being reconciled? Crave it? It's your body that dies, after all.

David Foster Wallace, "Federer as Religious Experience," *The New York Times*

This, then, is where the philosophic life begins, in a man's perception of the state of his ruling faculty [*aesthçsis tou idiou hçgemonikou pôs echei*]: for when once you realize that it is in a feeble state, you will not choose to employ it anymore for great matters. But, as it is, some men, finding themselves unable to swallow a mouthful, buy themselves a treatise, and set about eating it whole, and in consequence they vomit or have indigestion. Hence colics and fluxes and fevers. They ought first to have considered whether they have the faculty.

Epictetus, "I," *Discourses* (Translated from the Greek by Michel Foucault, "The Cultivation of the Self," *The Care of the Self: Volume 3 of the History of Sexuality*; Translated from the French by Robert Hurley)

Unable to Find What I Was Formerly Sure Was There

It is clear why the angels come no more.
Standing so large in their beautiful Latin,
how could they accept being refracted
so small in another grammar, or leave
their perfect singing for this broken speech?
Why should they stumble this alien world?

Jack Gilbert, "It Is Clear Why the Angels Come No More," *Views of Jeopardy*

May I, composed like them
Of Eros and of dust,
Beleaguered by the same
Negation and despair,
Show an affirming flame.

W.H. Auden, "September 1, 1939," *Another Time*

From the unseen horizon
and from the very center of my being,
an infinite voice pronounced these things—
things, not words. This is my feeble translation,
time-bound, of what was a single limitless Word:

"Stars, bread, libraries of East and West,
playing-cards, chessboards, galleries, skylights, cellars,
a human body to walk with on the earth,
fingernails, growing at nighttime and in death,
shadows for forgetting, mirrors busily multiplying,
cascades in music, gentlest of all time's shapes.
Borders of Brazil, Uruguay, horses and mornings,
a bronze weight, a copy of the Grettir Saga,
algebra and fire . . ."

Jorge Luis Borges (Translated by Alastair Reed), "Matthew XXV: 30,"
The Self and the Other

Julia Guez's poetry, essays, interviews and translations have appeared in *Poetry, The Guardian, PEN Poetry Series, The Kenyon Review, BOMB* and *The Brooklyn Rail.* She has been awarded the Discovery/*Boston Review* Poetry Prize, a Fulbright Fellowship and The John Frederick Nims Memorial Prize in Translation. Guez holds degrees from Rice and Columbia. For the last decade, she has worked with Teach For America; she's currently a managing director of programming there. She also teaches creative writing at Rutgers and writes poetry reviews for *Publishers Weekly.* Guez lives in Brooklyn and online at www.juliaguez.net.

Publication of this book was made possible by grants and donations. We are also grateful to those individuals who participated in our 2018 Build a Book Program. They are:

Anonymous (11), Vincent Bell, Jan Bender-Zanoni, Laurel Blossom, Adam Bohanon, Lee Briccetti, Jane Martha Brox, Carla & Steven Carlson, Andrea Cohen, Janet S. Crossen, Marjorie Deninger, Patrick Donnelly, Charles Douthat, Blas Falconer, Monica Ferrell, Joan Fishbein, Jennifer Franklin, Sarah Freligh, Helen Fremont & Donna Thagard, Robert Fuentes & Martha Webster, Ryan George, Panio Gianopoulos, Lauri Grossman, Julia Guez, Naomi Guttman & Jonathan Mead, Steven Haas, Bill & Cam Hardy, Lori Hauser, Ricardo Hernandez, Bill Holgate, Deming Holleran, Piotr Holysz, Nathaniel Hutner, Rebecca Kaiser Gibson, Voki Kalfayan, David Lee, Sandra Levine, Howard Levy, Owen Lewis, Jennifer Litt, Sara London & Dean Albarelli, David Long, Ralph & Mary Ann Lowen, Jacquelyn Malone, Fred Marchant, Louise Mathias, Catherine McArthur, Nathan McClain, Richard McCormick, Kamilah Aisha Moon, Beth Morris, Rebecca & Daniel Okrent, Jill Pearlman, Marcia & Chris Pelletiere, Maya Pindyck, Megan Pinto, Eileen Pollack, Barbara Preminger, Kevin Prufer, Martha Rhodes, Paula Rhodes, Linda Safyan, Peter & Jill Schireson, Jason Schneiderman, Roni & Richard Schotter, Jane Scovel, Andrew Seligsohn & Martina Anderson, Soraya Shalforoosh, Julie A. Sheehan, James Snyder & Krista Fragos, Alice St. Claire-Long, Megan Staffel, Dorothy Tapper Goldman, Marjorie & Lew Tesser, Boris Thomas, Connie Voisine, Calvin Wei, Bill Wenthe, Allison Benis White, Michelle Whittaker, Rachel Wolff, and Anton Yakovlev.

12/19

WITHDRAWN